MW00961917

# FROM HIM, THROUGH ME, TO YOU

MELINDA JONES SUTTON

Copyright © 2014 Melinda Jones Sutton

All rights reserved.

ISBN: 9798687537377

# DEDICATION

This book is dedicated to My Lord and Savior Jesus Christ. I honor you for trusting me during the time I could not see in front of me. You gave me eyes to see beyond my present condition and state of mind.

To those that helped me Brittany Payne Bruce, Genea Dukes, Tiffany Martin, Bryant Parker, and Sheena Thomas you are highly regarded. To the greatest church family on Earth: Divine Glory Ministries, Inc. for believing and supporting me.

# Table of Contents

From Him, Through Me, To You

# ACTIONS

**I must be willing to deal with the consequences of my actions without aborting the process of transformation.**

*For it is by grace you have been saved, through faith—and this is not from yourselves, it is the gift of God— not by works, so that no one can boast. For we are God's handiwork, created in Christ Jesus to do good works, which God prepared in advance for us to do.*

*Ephesians 2:8-10 NIV*

**After awakening from sleep, don't allow your dream to become the confirmation you seek.**

*Much dreaming and many words are meaningless. Therefore, fear God.*

*Ecclesiastes 5:7 NIV*

**Don't let your moment in time push you away from the promise.**

*And we also thank God continually because, when you received the word of God, which you heard from us, you accepted it not as a human word, but as it actually is, the word of God, which is indeed at work in you who believe.*

*Thessalonians 2:13 NIV*

**You can operate in empowerment dependent upon the source.**

*His divine power has given us everything we need for a godly life through our knowledge of him who called us by his own glory and goodness.*

*2 Peter 1:3 NIV*

**A moment on our lips is a lifetime on our souls. God is listening.**

*For the eyes of the Lord are on the righteous and his ears are attentive to their prayer, but the face of the Lord is against those who do evil.*

*1 Peter 3:12 NIV*

**When the word of God becomes your sustenance, you will know how to appropriately deal with yourself and life's issues.**

*Your word is a lamp for my feet, a light on my path.*

*Psalm 119:105 NIV*

**Your words have power to cultivate, sustain, and transform or they can act like poison.**

*Set a guard over my mouth, Lord; keep watch over the door of my lips.*

*Psalm 141:3 NIV*

**It's hard to do the wrong thing when the right thing is always on your mind.**

*Let us draw near to God with a sincere heart and with the full assurance that faith brings, having our hearts sprinkled to cleanse us from a guilty conscience and having our bodies washed with pure water.*

*Hebrews 10:22 NIV*

**There are things that will happen to you that you cannot control, but you can command your reaction.**

*For the Spirit God gave us does not make us timid, but gives us power, love, and self-discipline.*

*2 Timothy 1:7 NIV*

**Speak life over your dreams, declare victory over your weaknesses, and take action in those places you have given up on.**

*Do not let any unwholesome talk come out of your mouths, but only what is helpful for building others up according to their needs, that it may benefit those who listen.*

*Ephesians 4:29 NIV*

**Radical for Jesus – is really, no made up policy to circumvent.**

*I have been crucified with Christ and I no longer live, but Christ lives in me. The life I now live in the body, I live by faith in the Son of God, who loved me and gave himself for me.*

*Galatians 2:20 NIV*

**Speak life, when no life appears to be seen.**

*Truly I tell you, if anyone says to this mountain, Go, throw yourself into the sea, and does not doubt in their heart but believes that what they say will happen, it will be done for them.*

*Mark 11:23 NIV*

**Discontinue speaking about being thankful, while at the same time being angry for the things you wish you could have better.**

*My dear brothers and sisters, take note of this: Everyone should be quick to listen, slow to speak and slow to become angry, 20 because human anger does not produce the righteousness that God desires.*

*James 1:19-20 NIV*

# Notes

_____

_____

_____

_____

_____

_____

_____

_____

_____

_____

_____

_____

_____

_____

_____

_____

_____

_____

_____

_____

From Him, Through Me, To You

# ATTITUDE

**Your subconscious is the store house; It holds your true feelings, true desires, true motives, true thoughts, and your true weaknesses.**

*Finally, brothers, whatever is true, whatever is honorable, whatever is just, whatever is pure, whatever is lovely, whatever is commendable, if there is any excellence, if there is anything worthy of praise, think about these things.*

*Philippians 4:8 ESV*

**The most dangerous thing about having a distorted self-view is that your subconscious mind always works to prove your self-view concept true.**

*For by the grace given to me I say to everyone among you not to think of himself more highly than he ought to think, but to think with sober judgment, each according to the measure of faith that God has assigned.*

*Romans 12:3 ESV*

**If we don't or are unwilling to deal with our heart, we will continue in life seemly successful, but always running from truth, getting angry at those that present the truth, and improperly dealing with life, issues, relationships, and of course self.**

*Woe to those who are wise in their own eyes and clever in their own sight.*

*Isaiah 5:21 NIV*

## NO MORE GARBAGE THINKING...

*We demolish arguments and every pretension that sets itself up against the knowledge of God, and we take captive every thought to make it obedient to Christ.*

*2 Corinthians 10:5 NIV*

**Take off the superficial persona like you are so deep, only to recognize you are standing on a rocky terrain.**

*My eyes are on all their ways; they are not hidden from me, nor is their sin concealed from my eyes.*

*Jeremiah 16:17 NIV*

# Notes

_____

_____

_____

_____

_____

_____

_____

_____

_____

_____

_____

_____

_____

_____

_____

_____

_____

_____

_____

_____

_____

_____

_____

# BELIEVE

**Your belief system will set in motion your way of living.**

*For I know the plans I have for you, declares the Lord, plans to prosper you and not to harm you, plans to give you hope and a future.*

*Jeremiah 29:11 NIV*

**Remember you have victory in every area of your life; never allow what you are facing to shift your belief.**

*Even though I walk through the darkest valley, I will fear no evil, for you are with me; your rod and your staff, they comfort me. You prepare a table before me in the presence of my enemies. You anoint my head with oil; my cup overflows. Surely your goodness and love will follow me all the days of my life, and I will dwell in the house of the LORD forever.*

*Psalm 23:4-6 NIV*

**The War against manifestation is a war against the word. Continue to believe the promises of God because he has never lost a battle or lied.**

*So do not fear, for I am with you; do not be dismayed, for I am your God. I will strengthen you and help you; I will uphold you with my righteous right hand.*

*Isaiah 41:10 NIV*

**What are the unlimited possibilities that would release untapped abilities, talents, and gifting if you believed what God has spoken about you?**

*When you pass through the waters, I will be with you; and when you pass through the rivers, they will not sweep over you. When you walk through the fire, you will not be burned; the flames will not set you ablaze.*

*Isaiah 43:2 NIV*

**When you believe God, only then will you believe in His outcome.**

*For no matter how many promises God has made, they are "Yes" in Christ. And so through him the "Amen" is spoken by us to the glory of God.*

*2 Corinthians 1:20 NIV*

**What I believe to be true will determine my level of obedience towards God.**

*If any of you lacks wisdom, you should ask God, who gives generously to all without finding fault, and it will be given to you. But when you ask, you must believe and not doubt, because the one who doubts is like a wave of the sea, blown and tossed by the wind.*

*James 1:5-6 NIV*

**The belief system in which one exists by, will determine the logic of one's actions.**

*Follow my example, as I follow the example of Christ.*

*1 Corinthians 11:1 NIV*

**You have a future. Arise, believe, become, and take action.**

*And he said to them, "Go into all the world and proclaim the gospel to the whole creation. Whoever believes and is baptized will be saved, but whoever does not believe will be condemned."*

*Mark 16:15-16 ESV*

**Believe in who you are, thereby denouncing identity theft.**

*But you are a chosen people, a royal priesthood, a holy nation, God's special possession, that you may declare the praises of him who called you out of darkness into his wonderful light.*

*1 Peter 2:9 NIV*

**When you truly Believe in the promise, that belief will take away the fear, the voices of lies, that your dream or promise will never happen.**

*Be strong and courageous. Do not be afraid or terrified because of them, for the Lord your God goes with you; he will never leave you nor forsake you.*

*Deuteronomy 31:6 NIV*

# Notes

_____

_____

_____

_____

_____

_____

_____

_____

_____

_____

_____

_____

_____

_____

_____

_____

_____

_____

_____

_____

_____

_____

# BROKENNESS

**You were not created with brokenness, although you were created to endure brokenness.**

*So do not fear, for I am with you; do not be dismayed, for I am your God. I will strengthen you and help you; I will uphold you with my righteous right hand.*

*Isaiah 41:10 NIV*

**Brokenness doesn't mean without a solution. On the contrary, it's time for the manifestation of God's glory. Get ready for your miracle.**

*My flesh and my heart may fail, but God is the strength of my heart and my portion forever.*

*Psalm 73:26 NIV*

**God will use your broken pieces to propel you into greatness.**

*He said, "Can I not do with you, Israel, as this potter does?" declares the Lord. "Like clay in the hand of the potter, so are you in my hand, Israel."*

*Jeremiah 18:6 NIV*

**Broken things in our lives serve as opportunities, once we become willing to let God handle them.**

*We do not want you to be uninformed, brothers and sisters, about the troubles we experienced in the province of Asia. We were under great pressure, far beyond our ability to endure, so that we despaired of life itself. Indeed, we felt we had received the sentence of death. But this happened that we might not rely on ourselves but on God, who raises the dead. He has delivered us from such a deadly peril, and he will deliver us again. On him we have set our hope that he will continue to deliver us,*

*2 Corinthians 1:8-10 NIV*

**Operating out of a broken spirit will cause you to turn back on your word, it will cause you to deceive others; not to mention, sabotage someone else's destiny.**

*Sow righteousness for yourselves, reap the fruit of unfailing love, and break up your unplowed ground; for it is time to seek the Lord, until he comes and showers his righteousness on you.*

*Hosea 10:12 NIV*

**Operating out of a broken spirit will sabotage your reliability, have an effect on your judgment, and postpone your purpose.**

*Trust in the Lord with all your heart and lean not on your own understanding; in all your ways submit to him, and he will make your paths straight.*

*Proverbs 3:5-6 NIV*

## Notes

_____

_____

_____

_____

_____

_____

_____

_____

_____

_____

_____

_____

_____

_____

_____

_____

_____

_____

_____

_____

_____

# CHALLENGES

**If what you are facing signifies, "It's impossible", "It's Over", or "walk away"... take your hands off, and allow it to face your God, the God of All Capability.**

*For I am the Lord your God who takes hold of your right hand and says to you, Do not fear;*
*I will help you.*

*Isaiah 41:13 NIV*

**When what you are facing appears to be impossible, let your impossibilities become God's opportunity.**

*Do not be anxious about anything, but in every situation, by prayer and petition, with thanksgiving, present your requests to God.*

*Philippians 4:6 NIV*

**Walking away from difficulty is easy, the true test is remaining when difficulty is the test.**

*We are hard pressed on every side, but not crushed; perplexed, but not in despair; persecuted, but not abandoned; struck down, but not destroyed.*

*2 Corinthians 4:8-9 NIV*

**Do you have difficulty in reaching out or do you refuse to reach out beyond your difficulties?**

*I can do all this through him who gives me strength.*

*Philippians 4:13 NIV*

**The fight in front of you is not greater than the power within you.**

*And the God of all grace, who called you to his eternal glory in Christ, after you have suffered a little while, will himself restore you and make you strong, firm and steadfast.*

*1 Peter 5:10 NIV*

**Never Allow what you are facing to determine what you possess.**

*Cast all your anxiety on him because he cares for you.*

*1 Peter 5:7 NIV*

**Courage will change the emotional effect of challenges, while faith redirects your focus on the promise.**

*Be strong and courageous. Do not be afraid or terrified because of them, for the Lord your God goes with you; he will never leave you nor forsake you.*

*Deuteronomy 31:6 NIV*

**Cloudy days will happen, just remember the sun still takes it position.**

*To the one who is victorious, I will give the right to sit with me on my throne, just as I was victorious and sat down with my Father on his throne.*

*Revelation 3:21 NIV*

**When the complexity of life prompts you to give up, give in, to relocate, and break off, just remember, "who you are, will never be defeated to what you are experiencing".**

*The Lord will fight for you; you need only to be still.*

*Exodus 14:14 NIV*

**We fall down sometimes, but never out.**

*For no word from God will ever fail.*

*Luke 1:37 NIV*

**When you are facing life's challenges & testing, don't change your demeanor or your momentum.**

*Consider it pure joy, my brothers and sisters, whenever you face trials of many kinds, because you know that the testing of your faith produces perseverance. Let perseverance finish its work so that you may be mature and complete, not lacking anything.*

*James 1:2-4 NIV*

**If the path of possibilities is followed, the least likely chance of a person experiencing. The promises are not probable.**

*But thanks be to God! He gives us the victory through our Lord Jesus Christ.*

*1 Corinthians 15:57 NIV*

# Notes

# CHANGE

**When you choose to ignore, you relinquish your authority to change.**

*If we claim to be without sin, we deceive ourselves and the truth is not in us. If we confess our sins, he is faithful and just and will forgive us our sins and purify us from all unrighteousness.*

*1 John 1:8-9 NIV*

**You are greater than yesterday. As you walk into your today, remember it's a new day. Tomorrow is expecting to witness the manifestation of your change.**

*Therefore, if anyone is in Christ, the new creation has come: The old has gone, the new is here!*

*2 Corinthians 5:17 NIV*

**Transition is never opposition free!!! However, it is victory in advancement.**

*I press on toward the goal to win the prize for which God has called me heavenward in Christ Jesus.*

*Philippians 3:14 NIV*

**Change is essential from within!! If you are experiencing breaking, you are on course!!**

*Investigate my life, O God, find out everything about me; Cross-examine and test me, get a clear picture of what I'm about; See for yourself whether I've done anything wrong— then guide me on the road to eternal life.*

*Psalm 139:23-24 MSG*

**If you are experiencing a delay, it's only for continual transformation, shifting, and maturing, to receive your blessing.**

*For the revelation awaits an appointed time; it speaks of the end and will not prove false. Though it lingers, wait for it; it will certainly come and will not delay.*

*Habakkuk 2:3 NIV*

**The list of life deliberates, mistakes, or failures may be long, but those were the things that made you believe, caused a greater shift, rerouted your direction, produced a greater love for others, and strengthened you to stand and walk in Integrity.**

*And we know that God causes everything to work together for the good of those who love God and are called according to his purpose for them.*

*Romans 8:28 NLT*

**Change what you think and that will change your actions.**

*For as he thinketh in his heart, so is he:*

*Proverbs 23:7a KJV*

**You're being separated to eliminate all hazards. Your next level will not be contaminated.**

*Therefore, "Come out from them and be separate, says the Lord. Touch no unclean thing, and I will receive you."*

*2 Corinthians 6:17 NIV*

**Discontinue speaking about being thankful, while at the same time being angry for the things you wish you could have better.**

*Out of the same mouth come praise and cursing. My brothers and sisters, this should not be. Can both fresh water and salt water flow from the same spring? My brothers and sisters, can a fig tree bear olives, or a grapevine bear figs? Neither can a salt spring produce fresh water.*

*James 3:10-12 NIV*

# Notes

_____

_____

_____

_____

_____

_____

_____

_____

_____

_____

_____

_____

_____

_____

_____

_____

_____

_____

_____

_____

# CHARACTER

**Rising to the next level in ministry won't teach you how to be a man or woman of integrity, but it will certainly display what you are.**

*The servant who knows the master's will and does not get ready or does not do what the master wants will be beaten with many blows. But the one who does not know and does things deserving punishment will be beaten with few blows. From everyone who has been given much, much will be demanded; and from the one who has been entrusted with much, much more will be asked.*

*Luke 12:47-48 NIV*

**Remember that your true nature will put you on display, and then reveal the evidence.**

*The mind governed by the flesh is hostile to God; it does not submit to God's law, nor can it do so. Those who are in the realm of the flesh cannot please God.*

*Romans 8:7-8 NIV*

**The matters of the heart always surface. Keep it Clean.**

*The acts of the flesh are obvious: sexual immorality, impurity and debauchery; idolatry and witchcraft; hatred, discord, jealousy, fits of rage, selfish ambition, dissensions, factions and envy; drunkenness, orgies, and the like. I warn you, as I did before, that those who live like this will not inherit the kingdom of God.*

*Galatians 5:19-21 NIV*

**Never allow quitting to become your option, because that will develop your character and set ablaze trustworthiness.**

*But as for you, be strong and do not give up, for your work will be rewarded.*

*2 Chronicles 15:7 NIV*

**It takes courage to walk away or let go of anything that is attached to our flesh and not our divine destiny. Never allow the psychological snare of invested time to put your life in reverse.**

*Do not conform to the pattern of this world, but be transformed by the renewing of your mind. Then you will be able to test and approve what God's will is—his good, pleasing and perfect will.*

*Romans 12:2 NIV*

## Notes

_____

_____

_____

_____

_____

_____

_____

_____

_____

_____

_____

_____

_____

_____

_____

_____

_____

_____

_____

_____

_____

_____

_____

_____

# CONFLICT

**What disturbs you the most? Having to admit you were wrong or facing those you wronged?**

*Where do you think all these appalling wars and quarrels come from? Do you think they just happen? Think again. They come about because you want your own way, and fight for it deep inside yourselves.*

*James 4:1 MSG*

**God's love covered you in those places where self-sabotage worked at 100% to deny you access to your own next level.**

*But God demonstrates his own love for us in this: While we were still sinners, Christ died for us.*

*Romans 5:8 NIV*

**You are Greater than your conflict, pick yourself up & make a conscious decision to step into your liberation.**

*Yet to all who did receive him, to those who believed in his name, he gave the right to become children of God—*

*John 1:12 NIV*

**If you are being shaken, something must rise to the surface. Deal with it and move forward.**

*These trials will show that your faith is genuine. It is being tested as fire tests and purifies gold—though your faith is far more precious than mere gold. So when your faith remains strong through many trials, it will bring you much praise and glory and honor on the day when Jesus Christ is revealed to the whole world.*

*1 Peter 1:7 NLT*

**Remember this: God's word will never be at conflict with your visions.**

*Then the Lord said to me, "Write my answer plainly on tablets, so that a runner can carry the correct message to others.*

*Habakkuk 2:2 NLT*

**"The storm came, and my enemies evaluated my loss from a natural viewpoint; however, my load was only lightened so I could carry on.**

*Consider what God has done: Who can straighten what he has made crooked? When times are good, be happy; but when times are bad, consider this: God has made the one as well as the other. Therefore, no one can discover anything about their future.*

*Ecclesiastes 7:13-14 NIV*

# Notes

_____

_____

_____

_____

_____

_____

_____

_____

_____

_____

_____

_____

_____

_____

_____

_____

_____

_____

_____

_____

_____

_____

# CONNECTIONS

**Connect yourself with someone that understands the struggle, not those that struggle to understand.**

*Jesus answered, "I am the way and the truth and the life. No one comes to the Father except through me.*

*John 14:6 NIV*

**Friendship is a powerful relationship when the ingredients are free from deceit or fraud.**

*Therefore, since we are surrounded by such a great cloud of witnesses, let us throw off everything that hinders and the sin that so easily entangles. And let us run with perseverance the race marked out for us,*

*Hebrews 12:1 NIV*

**Never allow yourself to be seduced from divine connections.**

*Make my joy complete by being of the same mind, having the same love [toward one another], knit together in spirit, intent on one purpose [and living a life that reflects your faith and spreads the gospel—the good news regarding salvation through faith in Christ].*

*Philippians 2:2 AMP*

**Being genuine in a friendship eradicates all disguises.**

*Do not be misled: "Bad company corrupts good character."*

*1 Corinthians 15:33 NIV*

# Notes

# DECISIONS

**Remember, every decision you place into action will signify the Source of your reasoning.**

*Those who are dominated by the sinful nature think about sinful things, but those who are controlled by the Holy Spirit think about things that please the Spirit.*

*Romans 8:5 NLT*

**Forever is a long time. How will you spend it?**

*He will render to each one according to his works: to those who by patience in well-doing seek for glory and honor and immortality, he will give eternal life; but for those who are self-seeking and do not obey the truth, but obey unrighteousness, there will be wrath and fury.*

*Romans 2:6-8 (ESV)*

**Never allow the actions or decisions of an individual to draw you outside the will of God. What may appear to be right for others could mean entrapment and derailment from your destiny.**

*Therefore, my dear friends, as you have always obeyed—not only in my presence, but now much more in my absence—continue to work out your salvation with fear and trembling,*

*Philippians 2:12 NIV*

**When you won't make a decision, you will be pushed to a day of decision.**

*But if serving the Lord seems undesirable to you, then choose for yourselves this day whom you will serve, whether the gods your ancestors served beyond the Euphrates, or the gods of the Amorites, in whose land you are living. But as for me and my household, we will serve the Lord."*

*Joshua 24:15 NIV*

**Make the decision to declare greatness over your life, then create an atmosphere of worship, thereby causing your mind, body, and soul to embrace the new you.**

*Come, let us bow down in worship,*
*let us kneel before the Lord our Maker;*

*Psalm 95:6 NIV*

**Stop allowing your need to overshadow what you already have.**

*Consider the ravens: They do not sow or reap, they have no storeroom or barn; yet God feeds them. And how much more valuable you are than birds!*

*Luke 12:24 NIV*

**Make the decision that you will take the responsibility to love you!!!**

*Love endures with patience and serenity, love is kind and thoughtful, and is not jealous or envious; love does not brag and is not proud or arrogant. It is not rude; it is not self-seeking, it is not provoked [nor overly sensitive and easily angered]; it does not take into account a wrong endured.*

*1 Corinthians 13:4-5 AMP*

**Jesus is the source & resource choose to operate through Him.**

*The Lord is my shepherd, I lack nothing.*

*Psalm 23:1 NIV*

**Never allow the rebuttal of others to shatter your dreams.**

*But even if you should suffer for righteousness' sake, you will be blessed. Have no fear of them, nor be troubled,*

*1 Peter 3:14 ESV*

**Speak freedom from disastrous decision making, from a distorted understanding.**

[5] *Trust in the Lord with all thine heart; and lean not unto thine own understanding.*

*Proverbs 3:5 KJV*

**Make the decision to walk in His Perfect Love.**

*Such love has no fear, because perfect love expels all fear. If we are afraid, it is for fear of punishment, and this shows that we have not fully experienced his perfect love.*

*1 John 4:18 NLT*

**Never forget we are not without choices; however, use discernment and by doing    so you won't live a life of regrets.**

*Those who trust their own insight are foolish,
but anyone who walks in wisdom is safe.*

*Proverbs 28:26 NLT*

**Consequences of choices unfolding in an opportune time in life, will accelerate maturity.**

*Both the one who makes people holy and those who are made holy are of the same family. So Jesus is not ashamed to call them brothers and sisters.*

*Hebrews 2:11 NIV*

## Notes

_____

_____

_____

_____

_____

_____

_____

_____

_____

_____

_____

_____

_____

_____

_____

_____

_____

_____

_____

_____

_____

# DESIRES

**Thoughts will give life to desires, and desires will shape your future.**

*All of us used to live that way, following the passionate desires and inclinations of our sinful nature. By our very nature we were subject to God's anger, just like everyone else.*

*But God is so rich in mercy, and he loved us so much, that even though we were dead because of our sins, he gave us life when he raised Christ from the dead. (It is only by God's grace that you have been saved!)*

*Ephesians 2:3-5 NLT*

**Never allow what you want to minimize what You have already been Blessed with.**

*Do not wear yourself out to get rich;*
*do not trust your own cleverness.*

*Proverbs 23:4 NIV*

**Never allow your desires to override destiny, or you will spend years masquerading the role of God did it.**

*They will act religious, but they will reject the power that could make them godly. Stay away from people like that!*

*2 Timothy 3:5 NLT*

**Never allow your desires to become greater than the needs of others.**

*If anyone forces you to go one mile, go with them two miles.*

*Matthew 5:41 NIV*

**Never overlook that which you already possess.**

*...who gave himself for us to redeem us from all wickedness and to purify for himself a people that are his very own, eager to do what is good.*

*Titus 2:14 NIV*

**Unchecked desires will sabotage your life, reroute your direction, omit the consequences of your desires; it will cause a person to view truth, and deny ever knowing truth is reality.**

*Run from anything that stimulates youthful lusts. Instead, pursue righteous living, faithfulness, love, and peace. Enjoy the companionship of those who call on the Lord with pure hearts.*

*2 Timothy 2:22 NLT*

# Notes

# DESTINY

**When Jesus destined you for greater, He took away all joining possibilities that would collaborate against your destiny.**

*Also henceforth I am he;*
*there is none who can deliver from my hand;*
*I work, and who can turn it back?"*

*Isaiah 43:13 ESV*

**Next is designed to reflect your past, declare your present, and accelerate you into your destiny.**

*And having chosen them, he called them to come to him. And having called them, he gave them right standing with himself. And having given them right standing, he gave them his glory.*

*Romans 8:30 NLT*

**Your destiny is irrevocable, so whatever you give birth to will be healthy and blessed, or pre-mature and have years of tribulations.**

*Where can I go from Your Spirit?*
*Or where can I flee from Your presence?*

*Psalm 139:7 NKJV*

**Once God gives you a dream, the dream gives a free rein to achievement, at times it may appear difficult and even complicated, but it's your dream, It's still your destiny!!!**

*And the Lord answered me:*

*"Write the vision;*
*make it plain on tablets,*
*so he may run who reads it.*
*For still the vision awaits its appointed time;*
*it hastens to the end—it will not lie.*
*If it seems slow, wait for it;*
*it will surely come; it will not delay.*

*Habakkuk 2:2-3 ESV*

## Notes

_____

_____

_____

_____

_____

_____

_____

_____

_____

_____

_____

_____

_____

_____

_____

_____

_____

_____

_____

_____

_____

_____

_____

_____

_____

_____

_____

_____

_____

_____

_____

_____

_____

_____

_____

_____

_____

_____

_____

_____

_____

_____

_____

_____

# DEVELOPMENT

**Every Action does not require a reaction. Observation propels you into development.**

*But if you bite and devour one another, watch out that you are not consumed by one another.*

*But I say, walk by the Spirit, and you will not gratify the desires of the flesh.*

*Galatians 5:15-16 ESV*

**Where there is opportunity, there is development.**

*They go from strength to strength,*
*till each appears before God in Zion.*

*Psalm 84:7 NIV*

**When consequences are allowed to play out their role; you will no longer see adversity as dreadful, on the other hand, as development.**

*"For the Lord disciplines those he loves,*
*and he punishes each one he accepts as his child."*

*Hebrews 12:6 NLT*

**It is those necessary things in life that will accelerate your development and bring greater blessings in your life. Cease despising the necessary things and face your frustrations, hurts, loss, lies, relationships, and challenges.**

*My suffering was good for me,*
*for it taught me to pay attention to your decrees.*

*Psalm 119:71 NLT*

# Notes

_____

_____

_____

_____

_____

_____

_____

_____

_____

_____

_____

_____

_____

_____

_____

_____

_____

_____

_____

_____

_____

# DISCERNMENT

**Discernment is necessary when the obvious can't be recognized.**

*Uphold my steps in Your paths,*
*That my footsteps may not slip.*

*Psalm 17:5 NKJV*

**Never choose not to recognize reality, on the contrary, seek to discern the impossibility of what your heart and eyes can't understand.**

*For we live by believing and not by seeing.*

*2 Corinthians 5:7 NLT*

**Never forget, we are not without choices; however, use discernment and by doing so you won't live a life of regrets.**

*Those who trust their own insight are foolish,*
*but anyone who walks in wisdom is safe.*

*Proverbs 28:26 NLT*

## Notes

_____

_____

_____

_____

_____

_____

_____

_____

_____

_____

_____

_____

_____

_____

_____

_____

_____

_____

_____

_____

# EXPECTATIONS

**We become wounded in life because we expect more from people than what they are capable of accomplishing. Their lie becomes our pain and their failure becomes our object of mistrust.**

*"What is mankind that you make so much of them,
that you give them so much attention,"*

*Job 7:17 NIV*

**Never expect to lose, just be ready to reroute, adjust, and drop somethings.**

*In my distress I prayed to the Lord,
and the Lord answered me and set me free.*

*Psalm 118:5 NLT*

**Never envy the life of another; the maintenance of that life is not visible to you.**

*You desire but do not have, so you kill. You covet but you cannot get what you want, so you quarrel and fight. You do not have because you do not ask God.*

*James 4:2 NIV*

**Never envy the defiance of another that appears to be joyful and prospering.**

*Do not fret because of those who are evil or be envious of those who do wrong; ² for like the grass they will soon wither; like green plants they will soon die away. ³ Trust in the Lord and do good; dwell in the land and enjoy safe pasture.*

*Psalm 37: 1-3 NIV*

## Notes

_____

_____

_____

_____

_____

_____

_____

_____

_____

_____

_____

_____

_____

_____

_____

_____

_____

_____

_____

_____

# FAILURE

**Remember that failure is not an option, do not give it an opportunity in your life.**

*Have you been thinking all along that we have been defending ourselves to you? We have been speaking in the sight of God as those in Christ; and everything we do, dear friends, is for your strengthening.*

*2 Corinthians 12:19 NIV*

**Failure was never a part of the approved plan of God for your Life.**

*"For I know the plans I have for you," declares the Lord, "plans to prosper you and not to harm you, plans to give you hope and a future."*

*Jeremiah 29:11 NIV*

**The unspeakable failures lead you to being grateful for mini victories.**

*And we know that in all things God works for the good of those who love him, who have been called according to his purpose.*

*Romans 8:28 NIV*

## Notes

_____

_____

_____

_____

_____

_____

_____

_____

_____

_____

_____

_____

_____

_____

_____

_____

_____

_____

_____

_____

# FAITH

**Hold on to faith, the pain may increase, so will your anointing, your vision, and the realm in which you are called to operate in.**

*...fixing our eyes on Jesus, the pioneer and perfecter of faith. For the joy set before him he endured the cross, scorning its shame, and sat down at the right hand of the throne of God.*

*Hebrews 12:2 NIV*

**Remember a released word by faith will cause a "shift".**

*Jesus replied, "Truly I tell you, if you have faith and do not doubt, not only can you do what was done to the fig tree, but also you can say to this mountain, 'Go, throw yourself into the sea,' and it will be done.*

*Matthew 21:21 NIV*

**Faith, when allowed, will assert authority over your emotions and pain.**

*Resist him, standing firm in the faith, because you know that the family of believers throughout the world is undergoing the same kind of sufferings.*

*1 Peter 5:9 NIV*

**When I utilize Faith as my guide, I will no longer stagger, worry, or doubt, in areas that I should soar, live, and propel.**

*For we live by faith, not by sight.*

*2 Corinthians 5:7 NIV*

**Fear is overrated, while at the same time faith is being underestimated.**

*When I am afraid, I put my trust in you.*

*Psalm 56:3 NIV*

**When reasoning is in agreement with vision, is faith the foundation of your actions?**

*God is not man, that he should lie, or a son of man, that he should change his mind. Has he said, and will he not do it? Or has he spoken, and will he not fulfill it?*

*Numbers 23:19 ESV*

**A determined mind reflects faith.**

*They will perish, but you remain;
they will all wear out like a garment.*

*Hebrews 1:11 NIV*

**The source is the foundation of our Faith, thereby opening channels for you to obtain all resources you will need to be a successful disciple.**

*By faith we understand that the universe was formed at God's command, so that what is seen was not made out of what was visible.*

*Hebrews 11:3 NIV*

**Step out on faith, thereby allowing hope to carry you into your destiny.**

*And without faith it is impossible to please God, because anyone who comes to him must believe that he exists and that he rewards those who earnestly seek him.*

*Hebrews 11:6 NIV*

## Notes

_____

_____

_____

_____

_____

_____

_____

_____

_____

_____

_____

_____

_____

_____

_____

_____

_____

_____

_____

_____

# FORGIVENESS

**One of the most powerful prayers of liberation is when a heart of man chooses to leave behind his/her wounds, and declare forgiveness and blessings over their offender.**

*Bear with each other and forgive one another if any of you has a grievance against someone. Forgive as the Lord forgave you.*

*Colossians 3:13 NIV*

**Forgiveness is from a heart that can relate to mercy.**

*But if you do not forgive others their sins, your Father will not forgive your sins.*

*Matthew 6:15 NIV*

**Forgiveness is pressing beyond your pain to give someone your love. Ask Jesus. He's a great example of that.**

*For God so loved the world that he gave his one and only Son, that whoever believes in him shall not perish but have eternal life.*

*John 3:16 NIV*

**Forgiveness will only cost you your pride, but revenge will devastate your life.**

*And when you stand praying, if you hold anything against anyone, forgive them, so that your Father in heaven may forgive you your sins."*

*Mark 11:25 NIV*

## Notes

_____

_____

_____

_____

_____

_____

_____

_____

_____

_____

_____

_____

_____

_____

_____

_____

_____

_____

_____

_____

_____

# FREEDOM

**Unless you accept the love of Jesus Christ over your life and His word as absolute, it's impossible to walk in freedom.**

*I will walk about in freedom,*
*for I have sought out your precepts.*

*Psalm 119:45 NIV*


**Live with the confidence that Christ Jesus has set you free.**

*In him and through faith in him we may approach God with freedom and confidence.*

*Ephesians 3:12 NIV*


**Take pleasure in your freedom to live without boundaries, conquer without hesitation, operate without fear, and trust your creator wholeheartedly.**

*It is for freedom that Christ has set us free. Stand firm, then, and do not let yourselves be burdened again by a yoke of slavery.*

*Galatians 5:1 NIV*

**Freedom shifts!!**

*For the Lord is the Spirit, and wherever the Spirit of the Lord is, there is freedom.*

*2 Corinthians 3:17 NLT*

**One of the greatest attainments an individual can possess is the understanding of being set free.**

*But now that you have been set free from sin and have become slaves of God, the benefit you reap leads to holiness, and the result is eternal life.*

*Romans 6:22 NIV*

**Declaring freedom is powerful; however, living out your freedom is rewarding.**

*But whoever looks intently into the perfect law that gives freedom, and continues in it—not forgetting what they have heard, but doing it—they will be blessed in what they do.*

*James 1:25 NIV*

**Praying and reading your bible is not a substitute. However, it is the antidote needed to live out a life of freedom.**

*It is for freedom that Christ has set us free. Stand firm, then, and do not let yourselves be burdened again by a yoke of slavery.*

*Galatians 5:1 NIV*

**Loving myself doesn't mean issue free. However, it does mean free from poverty thinking, free from poverty living, and free from poverty connections.**

*If anyone thinks they are something when they are not, they deceive themselves.*

*Galatians 6:3 NIV*

**Freedom demands an atmosphere to display God's glory, God's power, and God's love.**

*"The Spirit of the Lord is on me,*
*because he has anointed me*
*to proclaim good news to the poor.*
*He has sent me to proclaim freedom for the prisoners*
*and recovery of sight for the blind,*
*to set the oppressed free,*

*Luke 4:18 NIV*

# Notes

# GOD'S WILL

**When God allows you to help someone discern their purpose, know your role. Don't confuse your gifting with God's Authority. Deny the spirit of control.**

*You, my brothers and sisters, were called to be free. But do not use your freedom to indulge the flesh; rather, serve one another humbly in love.*

*Galatians 5:13 NIV*

**We serve a God that takes the unfit, the unpromising, the worst of the worst, and uses them for his eternal holy purpose through His love.**

*Those who cleanse themselves from the latter will be instruments for special purposes, made holy, useful to the Master and prepared to do any good work.*

*2 Timothy 2:21 NIV*

**Before you initiate praying against what is happening to you, ask God for understanding first. It may be a part of His divine will for your life.**

*I keep asking that the God of our Lord Jesus Christ, the glorious Father, may give you the Spirit of wisdom and revelation, so that you may know him better.*

*Ephesians 1:17 NIV*

**Your hearing accurately positions you to receive instructions so that you're able to live out God's divine will for your life.**

*"Therefore everyone who hears these words of mine and puts them into practice is like a wise man who built his house on the rock.*

*Matthew 7:24 NIV*

**God's Plan for your life is far greater than you, wishing for things to get better, be better, and to turn out for your good.**

*For I know the plans I have for you," declares the Lord, "plans to prosper you and not to harm you, plans to give you hope and a future.*

*Jeremiah 29:11 NIV*

**Rejoice! His will is your victory in every battle, promise in the face of uncertainty, & provision for every divine assignment.**

*Yet in all these things we are more than conquerors and gain an overwhelming victory through Him who loved us [so much that He died for us].*

*Romans 8:37 AMP*

**The good pleasure of God's will will strip away the false hope of this world.**

*Do not conform to the pattern of this world, but be transformed by the renewing of your mind. Then you will be able to test and approve what God's will is—his good, pleasing, and perfect will.*

*Romans 12:2 NIV*

**Ultimately, God's promises are to advance His will and to let us know what He is doing.**

*All Scripture is God-breathed and is useful for teaching, rebuking, correcting, and training in righteousness, that the servant of God may be thoroughly equipped for every good work.*

*2 Timothy 3:16-17 NIV*

**Giving God the control doesn't mean things will become out of control, it just means you have no say-so on the outcome.**

*Trust in the Lord with all your heart*
*and lean not on your own understanding;*
*in all your ways submit to him,*
*and he will make your paths straight.*

*Proverbs 3:5-6 NIV*

**God's gifts for you brings blessings. When we reject God's gifts for the appearance of something or someone better, we are accepting the responsibility of working to maintain them.**

*The blessing of the Lord, it marketh rich, and he addeth no sorrow with it.*

*Proverbs 10:22 KJV*

**God is simply waiting to use it all for your recovery, return, and your next level.**

*And we know [with great confidence] that God [who is deeply concerned about us] causes all things to work together [as a plan] for good for those who love God, to those who are called according to His plan and purpose.*

*Romans 8:28 AMP*

**The path that is chosen may Appear to Be God's perfect will; it is sometimes the path that is needed to obtain His perfect will.**

*Enter through the narrow gate. For wide is the gate and broad is the road that leads to destruction, and many enter through it.*

*Matthew 7:13 NIV*

**Remember, If God has approved it, you will not have to develop it.**

*For all the promises of God in Him are Yes, and in Him Amen, to the glory of God through us.*

*2 Corinthians 1:20 NKJV*

# Notes

_____

_____

_____

_____

_____

_____

_____

_____

_____

_____

_____

_____

_____

_____

_____

_____

_____

_____

_____

_____

# GREATER

**I speak that God's anointing and gifting propel me into my next.**

*A man's gift makes room for him
and brings him before the great.*

*Proverbs 18:16  ESV*

**I declare that the anointing and gifting that has been placed upon my life will cause a shift in the earth realm.**

*But you have an anointing from the Holy One, and all of you know the truth.*

*1 John 2:20 NIV*

**It is between the space of the beginning and end, where your past and present met for new possibilities!!!**

*This means that anyone who belongs to Christ has become a new person. The old life is gone; a new life has begun!*

*2 Corinthians 5:17 NLT*

**Dream beyond your present circumstances, embrace greater, and then begin making decisions as if you have already attained it.**

*I press on toward the goal to win the prize for which God has called me heavenward in Christ Jesus.*

*Philippians 3:14 NIV*

**Embrace the will of God with an expectation that your life will never look like your desires but will the replica of greatness.**

*For I know the plans I have for you," declares the Lord, "plans to prosper you and not to harm you, plans to give you hope and a future.*

*Jeremiah 29:11 NIV*

**God has set you in motion for divine greatness.**

*Surely, Lord, you bless the righteous;*
*you surround them with your favor as with a shield.*

*Psalm 5:12 NIV*

**What more can Jesus do for you? How can He Prove to You that He positioned you for greater?**

*For the Lord God is a sun and shield;*
*the Lord bestows favor and honor;*
*no good thing does he withhold*
*from those whose walk is blameless.*

*Psalm 84:11 NIV*

**Whenever you need a little self-esteem boost, turn back through the pages of your own story. You didn't just survive; you became greater.**

*No, in all these things we are more than conquerors through him who loved us.*

*Romans 8:37 NIV*

**Don't despise who I am now. God is not finished using the lumps in my life to accelerate me to greater.**

*Yet you, Lord, are our Father.*
*We are the clay, you are the potter;*
*we are all the work of your hand.*

*Isaiah 64:8 NIV*

**If you have been broken for use, you were interrupted for greater.**

*Those who cleanse themselves from the latter will be instruments for special purposes, made holy, useful to the Master and prepared to do any good work.*

*2 Timothy 2:21 NIV*

**God is ever ready to move you to the next level, deny being comfortable in the same places, doing the same things!! Dare to dream, dare to hope, dare to be successful, dare to be first.**

*Commit to the Lord whatever you do,*
*and he will establish your plans.*

*Proverbs 16:3 NIV*

**See the greater within you.**

*You, dear children, are from God and have overcome them, because the one who is in you is greater than the one who is in the world.*

*1 John 4:4 NIV*

**The facts are against you; however, the facts are not final!!!
There is greater waiting for you.**

*No, despite all these things, overwhelming victory is ours through
Christ, who loved us.*

*Romans 8:37 NLT*

## Notes

_____

_____

_____

_____

_____

_____

_____

_____

_____

_____

_____

_____

_____

_____

_____

_____

_____

_____

_____

_____

_____

# HONESTY

**My responsibility to myself is to be honest, my responsibility for others is to respond from it.**

*Search me, God, and know my heart;*
*test me and know my anxious thoughts.*
*See if there is any offensive way in me,*
*and lead me in the way everlasting.*

*Psalm 139:23-24 NIV*


**Honesty with one's self will always cause an honest evaluation regarding one's self.**

*"Then you will know the truth, and the truth will set you free."*

*John 8:32 NIV*


**Honesty is spoken through love when there is nothing to gain.**

*Jesus Christ is the same yesterday and today and forever.*

*Hebrews 13:8 NIV*

# Notes

_____

_____

_____

_____

_____

_____

_____

_____

_____

_____

_____

_____

_____

_____

_____

_____

_____

_____

_____

# HOPE

**Hope speaks to our false labor pains with certainty of - there is a 'GOD' expected end.**

*For our light and momentary troubles are achieving for us an eternal glory that far outweighs them all.*

*2 Corinthians 4:17 NIV*

**Hope encourages us to see & hold on before the actual manifestation, in God's view point of an expected end, not ours.**

*..but those who hope in the Lord*
*will renew their strength.*
*They will soar on wings like eagles;*
*they will run and not grow weary,*
*they will walk and not be faint.*

*Isaiah 40:31 NIV*

**Hope declares God's word to be absolute over our future.**

*The Lord will keep you from all harm—*
*he will watch over your life;*
*the Lord will watch over your coming and going*
*both now and forevermore.*

*Psalm 121:7-8 NIV*

# Notes

_____

_____

_____

_____

_____

_____

_____

_____

_____

_____

_____

_____

_____

_____

_____

_____

_____

_____

_____

_____

_____

_____

# INTEGRITY

**Remember this, integrity will speak for you if you stop trying to defend yourself.**

*keeping a clear conscience, so that those who speak maliciously against your good behavior in Christ may be ashamed of their slander.*

*1 Peter 3:16 NIV*

**Encourage someone you know that has walked in integrity in the face of adversity.**

*Blessed is the one who perseveres under trial because, having stood the test, that person will receive the crown of life that the Lord has promised to those who love him.*

*James 1:12 NIV*

**What is your word worth? When you strip a Man (or Woman) down to nothing the only thing you have left is Your Word.**

*The tongue has the power of life and death, and those who love it will eat its fruit.*

*Proverbs 18:21 NIV*

**If you walk in integrity, you will never have to apologize for your actions.**

*The path of the righteous is level;*
*you, the Upright One, make the way of the righteous smooth.*

*Isaiah 26:7 NIV*

## Notes

_____

_____

_____

_____

_____

_____

_____

_____

_____

_____

_____

_____

_____

_____

_____

_____

_____

_____

_____

_____

_____

# INTERFERENCE

**There is nothing immoral about enjoying life, as long as that life does not cause you to miss the call, instructions, and warnings of God.**

*Therefore, I urge you, brothers and sisters, in view of God's mercy, to offer your bodies as a living sacrifice, holy and pleasing to God—this is your true and proper worship.*

*Romans 12:1 NIV*

**Life will illuminate insignificant issues in order to shift you away from your divine assignment. Allow God to handle your insignificants, thereby remaining the course.**

*Mark out a straight path for your feet;*
*stay on the safe path.*

*Proverbs 4:26 NLT*

**Never allow the actions of another to cause you to withdraw from your assignment!!**

*So then, each of us will give an account of ourselves to God.*

*Romans 14:12 NIV*

**God has legal right to interfere with distorted emotions, thoughts, and spoken words, that seek to download into your destiny.**

*To him who is able to keep you from stumbling and to present you before his glorious presence without fault and with great joy—*

*Jude 1: 24 NIV*

**Satisfaction if allowed to rule will eventually destroy who you were created to be.**

*Temptation comes from our own desires, which entice us and drag us away.*

*James 1:14 NLT*

**Remember you are of great value for the kingdom. The warfare you are experiencing is real. It comes to shake the foundation of your confidence. However, the outcome has already been determined. Stay on course.**

*For we are God's handiwork, created in Christ Jesus to do good works, which God prepared in advance for us to do.*

*Ephesians 2:10 NIV*

**One may see conflicting evidence, however, never become shaken or doubtful about the outcome.**

*Truly he is my rock and my salvation;*
*he is my fortress, I will never be shaken.*

*Psalm 62:6 NIV*

# Notes

_____

_____

_____

_____

_____

_____

_____

_____

_____

_____

_____

_____

_____

_____

_____

_____

_____

_____

_____

_____

_____

_____

# LETTING GO

**We have the greatest example of letting go, Jesus!!**

*Who, being in very nature God,*
*did not consider equality with God something to be used to his*
*own advantage;*
*rather, he made himself nothing*
*by taking the very nature of a servant,*
*being made in human likeness.*
*And being found in appearance as a man,*
*he humbled himself*
*by becoming obedient to death—*
*even death on a cross!*

*Philippians 2:6-8 NIV*

**Letting go of my past is the beginning of my future.**

*"Brothers and sisters, I do not consider myself yet to have taken*
*hold of it. But one thing I do: Forgetting what is behind and*
*straining toward what is ahead..."*

*Philippians 3:13 NIV*

**He knows where you are, the issue becomes problematic when you refuse to let go of the chaos to walk in His Perfect Love.**

*Submit yourselves, then, to God. Resist the devil, and he will flee from you.*

*James 4:7 NIV*

**Let go of who's not on board with your dream and get on board with destiny.**

*The Lord will fulfill his purpose for me;*
*your steadfast love, O Lord, endures forever.*
*Do not forsake the work of your hands.*

*Psalm 138:8 ESV*

**Name it & throw it!!! Don't go back and retrieve it!!!**

*As a dog returns to its vomit,*
*so fools repeat their folly.*

*Proverbs 26:11 NIV*

**It's an invaluable human ability to keep reviewing our mistakes over and over, re-experiencing the same negative emotions that tend to keep us stuck in negativity. The solution is not denial or distraction, just simply letting go & moving forward.**

*Trust in the Lord with all your heart*
*and lean not on your own understanding;*
*in all your ways submit to him,*
*and he will make your paths straight.*

*Proverbs 3:5-6 NIV*

**Let go of who is responsible and be willing to open your heart to God, only then can you let God fix It.**

*Do not be anxious about anything, but in every situation, by prayer and petition, with thanksgiving, present your requests to God. And the peace of God, which transcends all understanding, will guard your hearts and your minds in Christ Jesus.*

*Philippians 4:6-7 NIV*

**When you become so entangled with the affairs, issues, and concerns of life, it will consume your very being. Let Go & Relax, there is a plan that has already been designed to handle all of it for You!!**

*Keep reminding God's people of these things. Warn them before God against quarreling about words; it is of no value, and only ruins those who listen.*

*2 Timothy 2:14 NIV*

**Enjoy your life by letting your mind rest from those things that may never happen. Let go of all your worries.**

*Give all your worries and cares to God, for he cares about you.*

*1 Peter 5:7 NLT*

**When I let go of what I am, I become what I was designed to be. When I let go of what I have, I receive what I need.**

*"I am the vine; you are the branches. If you remain in me and I in you, you will bear much fruit; apart from me you can do nothing."*

*John 15:5 NIV*

**You may not have had to go through drastic changes in life. However, we all face the dilemma of letting go and holding on.**

*Then he said to them all: "Whoever wants to be my disciple must deny themselves and take up their cross daily and follow me.*

*Luke 9:23 NIV*

## Notes

_____

_____

_____

_____

_____

_____

_____

_____

_____

_____

_____

_____

_____

_____

_____

_____

_____

_____

_____

_____

_____

_____

# LIFESTYLE

**How you handle life and issues, will determine the life that you live.**

*"I have told you these things, so that in me you may have peace. In this world you will have trouble. But take heart! I have overcome the world."*

*John 16:33 NIV*

**You can never stop anyone from false accusation; however, you can live a life to make them out of a liar.**

*As a prisoner for the Lord, then, I urge you to live a life worthy of the calling you have received.*

*Ephesians 4:1 NIV*

**Never allow your life to reflect brokenness, but rather let your life speak from willingness.**

*As a prisoner for the Lord, then, I urge you to live a life worthy of the calling you have received.*

*Ephesians 4:1 NIV*

**What is taking place in your life that will create a God Delivery and not a human desire delivery?**

*For my thoughts are not your thoughts, neither are your ways my ways, declares the Lord. For as the heavens are higher than the earth, so are my ways higher than your ways and my thoughts than your thoughts.*

*Isaiah 55: 8-9 NIV*

**Create a standard for your life to eliminate all possibilities with the appearance of opportunities - that are sent to set you up with life altering emotions, desires, love, and dreams - to damage your destiny.**

*Do not conform to the pattern of this world, but be transformed by the renewing of your mind. Then you will be able to test and approve what God's will is—his good, pleasing, and perfect will.*

*Romans 12:2 NIV*

**Remember that your life will display who you are connected with.**

*Do not be misled: "Bad company corrupts good character."*

*1 Corinthians 15:33 NIV*

**Probable or promise; which path will display your choices in life?**

*"I have the right to do anything," you say—but not everything is beneficial. "I have the right to do anything"—but I will not be mastered by anything.*

*1 Corinthians 6:12 NIV*

**Encourage someone: Let your life be an example of change.**

*In the same way, let your light shine before others, that they may see your good deeds and glorify your Father in heaven.*

*Matthew 5:16 NIV*

**God never intended for you to hold onto life. On the contrary, He created you to live a life that will cause life to honor you. Stop holding on. Let Go and Live.**

*The thief cometh not, but for to steal, and to kill, and to destroy: I am come that they might have life, and that they might have it more abundantly.*

*John 10:10 KJV*

**We don't want to be characterized by the world just the notoriety of it.**

*Do not conform to the pattern of this world, but be transformed by the renewing of your mind. Then you will be able to test and approve what God's will is—his good, pleasing, and perfect will.*

*Romans 12:2 NIV*

## Notes

_____

_____

_____

_____

_____

_____

_____

_____

_____

_____

_____

_____

_____

_____

_____

_____

_____

_____

_____

_____

_____

_____

_____

# LIMITATIONS

**Whoever spoke "Limitations" over your life was only trying to dismantle your belief in God's Promises concerning your destiny.**

*However, as it is written:*
*"What no eye has seen, what no ear has heard,*
*and what no human mind has conceived"—*
*the things God has prepared for those who love him—*

*1 Corinthians 2:9 NIV*

**Disallow, renounce and deny every limitation.**

*I can do all this through him who gives me strength.*

*Philippians 4:13 NIV*

**If you want to remove limitations from your life, your first step is to remove: your "Will" which is attached to your inner desires, premature words spoken over your life, and false words released into your life.**

*Then he said to them all: "Whoever wants to be my disciple must deny themselves and take up their cross daily and follow me.*

*Luke 9:23 NIV*

# Notes

_____

_____

_____

_____

_____

_____

_____

_____

_____

_____

_____

_____

_____

_____

_____

_____

_____

_____

_____

_____

# LOVE

**If you love yourself with the love of Jesus, then you can properly love others without selfish motives, selfish gain, or selfish intent.**

*It does not dishonor others, it is not self-seeking, it is not easily angered, it keeps no record of wrongs.*

*1 Corinthians 13:5 NIV*

**When LOVE motivates us to follow JESUS, obedience is joyful not drudgery!**

*Jesus replied: "'Love the Lord your God with all your heart and with all your soul and with all your mind.'*

*Matthew 22:37 NIV*

**His love forgives, protects, comforts, directs, redeems, and matures as we walk in His divine will.**

*The Lord appeared to us in the past, saying: "I have loved you with an everlasting love;*
*I have drawn you with unfailing kindness.*

*Jeremiah 31:3 NIV*

**The mere fact that "you" made it "through" demonstrates God's love for "you".**

*But God demonstrates his own love for us in this: While we were still sinners, Christ died for us.*

*Romans 5:8 NIV*

**Can "YOU" Love "YOURSELF" without the love of anyone "Else"? Too often we rely on the love and affection of another without knowing how to function in loving "SELF".**

*I praise you because I am fearfully and wonderfully made;*
*your works are wonderful,*
*I know that full well.*

*Psalm 139:14 NIV*

**"When you are genuinely loved, you never have to seek for approval because that LOVE "Has APPROVED YOU", Trust the Love that Trusts You".**

*Greater love has no one than this: to lay down one's life for one's friends.*

*John 15:13 NIV*

### *CAN You Genuinely Love Beyond Your Pain?*

*And we know that in all things God works for the good of those who love him, who have been called according to his purpose.*

*Romans 8:28 NIV*

## When there is self "Love", it will create a standard for the response of love from others.

*So in everything, do to others what you would have them do to you, for this sums up the Law and the Prophets.*

*Matthew 7:12 NIV*

## Love is powerful, so we must use it accordingly towards self and others.

*So in everything, do to others what you would have them do to you, for this sums up the Law and the Prophets.*

*Matthew 7:12 NIV*

**We put up "walls" to deny dealing with life 's hurts and failures. God uses the wall to plant a "vinyl called "love". Love covered "YOU" to deny hate from killing "purpose" within "YOU".**

*Above all, love each other deeply, because love covers over a multitude of sins.*

*1 Peter 4:8 NIV*

**To be a world changer, one must "Love" unconditionally, without assimilation.**

*Do everything in love.*

*1 Corinthians 16:14 NIV*

**There is no greater opportunity at "Love" than YOURSELF!!!! It will be extremely difficult to give to another, what you are unable to attain for "Yourself".**

*Love must be sincere. Hate what is evil; cling to what is good.*

*Romans 12:9 NIV*

**A person can only resemble a "Love" that he or she "Comprehends".**

*Whoever does not love does not know God, because God is love.*

*1 John 4:8 NIV*

**Treat someone today with "Unconditional Love & Forgiveness", even if that person is 'Yourself'.**

*Above all, love each other deeply, because love covers over a multitude of sins.*

*1 Peter 4:8 NIV*

**The Love of Jesus will cause you to love others and at the same time, does not blind you.**

*Anyone who loves their brother and sister lives in the light, and there is nothing in them to make them stumble.*

*1 John 2:10 NIV*

**L.O.V.E. Only requires a response from L.O.V.E.**

*Do everything in love.*

*1 Corinthians 16:14 NIV*

# Notes

_____

_____

_____

_____

_____

_____

_____

_____

_____

_____

_____

_____

_____

_____

_____

_____

_____

_____

_____

_____

_____

# MINDSET

**In order to achieve, one must never begin with a defeated mindset and life's what ifs...**

*Commit to the Lord whatever you do,*
*and he will establish your plans.*

*Proverbs 16:3 NIV*

**Achievement of any task must begin with a mindset.**

*Therefore, preparing your minds for action, and being sober-minded, set your hope fully on the grace that will be brought to you at the revelation of Jesus Christ.*

*1 Peter 1:13 ESV*

**Laughter does the heart well!!! Laugh!!! Refuse to be saddened by those things out of your control and those things you think are in your control, "Laugh"; Free your mind!!!**

*A wicked man taketh a gift out of the bosom to pervert the ways of judgment.*

*Proverbs 17:23 KJV*

**Enjoy "Your Life" by letting your mind rest from those things that may never happen; let go of all your worries**

*And which of you with taking thought can add to his stature one cubit? If ye then be not able to do that thing which is least, why take ye thought for the rest?*

*Luke 12:25-26 KJV*

# Notes

# MISTAKES

**The biggest mistake you can make in life is always "fearing" you will make a mistake.**

*For I am the Lord your God*
*who takes hold of your right hand*
*and says to you, Do not fear;*
*I will help you.*

*Isaiah 41:13 NIV*

**I Choose not to weep over my fault, nor will I wish it never happened. However, I will use my mistakes to embrace my destiny.**

*Brothers and sisters, I do not consider that I have made it my own yet; but one thing I do: forgetting what lies behind and reaching forward to what lies ahead, I press on toward the goal to win the [heavenly] prize of the upward call of God in Christ Jesus.*

*Philippians 3:13-14 AMP*

## God will use your Error to re-define your Destiny...

*And we know that in all things God works for the good of those who love him, who have been called according to his purpose.*

*Romans 8:28 NIV*

# Notes

_____

_____

_____

_____

_____

_____

_____

_____

_____

_____

_____

_____

_____

_____

_____

_____

_____

_____

_____

_____

_____

# MOVING FORWARD

**Move from the place of "garbage thinking & emotions", "poverty minded relationships", "redundant expectations", and "Destructive behavior patterns".**

*You were taught, with regard to your former way of life, to put off your old self, which is being corrupted by its deceitful desires; to be made new in the attitude of your minds; and to put on the new self, created to be like God in true righteousness and holiness.*

*Ephesians 4:22-24 NIV*

**Next is the by-product of the previous experience you had to go through in order to be called to another position.**

*Not only so, but we also glory in our sufferings, because we know that suffering produces perseverance; perseverance, character; and character, hope. And hope does not put us to shame, because God's love has been poured out into our hearts through the Holy Spirit, who has been given to us.*

*Romans 5:3-5 NIV*

### "STOP LOOKING BACK AT YESTERDAY"!!

*Let your eyes look straight ahead;*
*fix your gaze directly before you.*

*Proverbs 4:25 NIV*

**If Jesus has declared "Next" in your life... That thing or person was not a loss, just part of your "Resume".**

*See, I am doing a new thing!*
*Now it springs up; do you not perceive it?*
*I am making a way in the wilderness*
*and streams in the wasteland.*

*Isaiah 43:19 NIV*

**Yesterday is in His hands, leave all your deliberates, mistakes, and failures, and embrace a Loving and Concerned Father.**

*"...casting all your cares [all your anxieties, all your worries, and all your concerns, once and for all] on Him, for He cares about you [with deepest affection, and watches over you very carefully]."*

*1 Peter 5:7 AMP*

## WHAT DO YOU BELIEVE ABOUT YOUR "NEXT"?

*But as it is written: "Eye has not seen, nor ear heard, Nor
have entered into the heart of man
The things which God has prepared for those who love Him."*

*1 Corinthians 2:9 NKJV*

**Declaring and Confirming God's word over our lives is the
beginning. The Next level is to open yourself "for" that
which you declare and confirm.**

*"...so shall my word be that goes out from my mouth;
it shall not return to me empty,
but it shall accomplish that which I purpose,
and shall succeed in the thing for which I sent it."*

*Isaiah 55:11 ESV*

**Stepping into "Your" new Season may appear that you are leaving others behind, in reality you are an example of triumph.**

*But whatever were gains to me I now consider loss for the sake of Christ. What is more, I consider everything a loss because of the surpassing worth of knowing Christ Jesus my Lord, for whose sake I have lost all things. I consider them garbage, that I may gain Christ*

*Philippians 3:7-8 NIV*

**Never go backwards in order to feel comfortable, instead, keep moving forward in difficult Circumstance, that will accelerate you for Purpose.**

*Another also said, "I will follow You, Lord [as Your disciple]; but first let me say goodbye to those at my home." But Jesus said to him, "No one who puts his hand to the plow and looks back [to the things left behind] is fit for the kingdom of God."*

*Luke 9:61-62 AMP*

**When the "end" has been declared, never look for your beginning to have anything from your previous life attached to it.**

*Therefore, if anyone is in Christ, the new creation has come: The old has gone, the new is here!*

*2 Corinthians 5:17 NIV*

**At the end of all things is the beginning of another. Allow new discoveries, self-reflections, and future considerations.**

*Your beginnings will seem humble,*
*so prosperous will your future be.*

*Job 8:7 NIV*

**The preparation for your next level is not always obvious, just beneficial.**

*Beloved, do not think it strange concerning the fiery trial which is to try you, as though some strange thing happened to you; ᵇᵘᵗ rejoice to the extent that you partake of Christ's sufferings, that when His glory is revealed, you may also be glad with exceeding joy.*

*1 Peter 4:12-13 NKJV*

**You have been weeping over your loss, let your loss weep over you.**

*Therefore, there is now no condemnation for those who are in Christ Jesus,*

*Romans 8:1 NIV*

**Don't allow your steps to become familiar with your past.**

*But Lot's wife looked back, and she became a pillar of salt.*

*Genesis 19:26 NIV*

**Discontinue the attempts to circumvent around and go through.**

*"Forget the former things;*
*do not dwell on the past.*

*Isaiah 43:18 NIV*

**My past was a moment ago and my future is NOW!!!**

*Let your eyes look straight ahead;*
*fix your gaze directly before you.*

*Proverbs 4:25 NIV*

**Leave your past behind and position yourself for a Greater Future.**

*Forget the former things;*
*do not dwell on the past.*

*Isaiah 43:18 NIV*

# Notes

# OBSTACLES

**The rain that is happening in your life is not there to drown you, on the contrary, it is there to perfect movement in your life. Arise and become "Greater".**

*Consider it pure joy, my brothers and sisters, whenever you face trials of many kinds, because you know that the testing of your faith produces perseverance. Let perseverance finish its work so that you may be mature and complete, not lacking anything.*

*James 1:2-4 NIV*

**Every now and then, life throws us in the deep ends and tells us to swim.**

*I was pushed back and about to fall,*
*but the Lord helped me.*

*Psalm 118:13 NIV*

**The next time you find yourself facing a giant – tell your giant, "thank you" for the momentum.**

*As the Philistine moved closer to attack him, David ran quickly toward the battle line to meet him.*

*1 Samuel 17:48 NIV*

**Facing obstacles doesn't mean you are not "favored".**

*Blessed is the one who perseveres under trial because, having stood the test, that person will receive the crown of life that the Lord has promised to those who love him.*

*James 1:12 NIV*

**Never allow a closed door to frustrate you or propel you into a place of despair. Only discernment knows when you are being protected or denied by the closed door.**

*And we know that in all things God works for the good of those who love him, who have been called according to his purpose.*

*Romans 8:28 NIV*

**We may face heartbreaking blows – but never damaged goods.**

*Already you have all you want! Already you have become rich! You have begun to reign—and that without us! How I wish that you really had begun to reign so that we also might reign with you! For it seems to me that God has put us apostles on display at the end of the procession, like those condemned to die in the arena. We have been made a spectacle to the whole universe, to angels as well as to human beings.*

*1 Corinthians 4:8-9 NIV*

**When doubt, fear, warfare, lies, and inner voices attempt to shift you from "your promise", just remember, "Your declared word is God's Promises".**

*Your kingdom is an everlasting kingdom,*
*and your dominion endures through all generations. The Lord is*
*trustworthy in all he promises*
*and faithful in all he does.*

*Psalm 145:13 NIV*

**Never allow the blocked doors of past plans to bring you to a standstill.**

*"Say to them, 'This is what the Lord says: "'When people fall down, do they not get up? When someone turns away, do they not return?*

*Jeremiah 8:4 NIV*

# Notes

_____

_____

_____

_____

_____

_____

_____

_____

_____

_____

_____

_____

_____

_____

_____

_____

_____

_____

_____

_____

_____

# PAIN

**Don't abort what God has said because of the pain, "besides after this is over ", you won't remember the pain, only the process.**

*I consider that our present sufferings are not worth comparing with the glory that will be revealed in us.*

*Romans 8:18 NIV*

**Pain has the tendency of reminding you and I of the significant things in life and who really cares.**

*Then I would still have this consolation—*
*my joy in unrelenting pain—*
*that I had not denied the words of the Holy One.*

*Job 6:10 NIV*

## Notes

_____

_____

_____

_____

_____

_____

_____

_____

_____

_____

_____

_____

_____

_____

_____

_____

_____

_____

_____

_____

_____

_____

_____

_____

_____

_____

_____

# PERCEPTION

**"Your perception of "self" will manifest through your daily routine. Reroute."**

*"...for he is the kind of person*
*who is always thinking about the cost.*
*"Eat and drink," he says to you,*
*but his heart is not with you.*

*Proverbs 23:7 NIV*

**"When the Perception of myself" is transformed, then my Value Increases."**

*Do not conform to the pattern of this world, but be transformed by the renewing of your mind. Then you will be able to test and approve what God's will is—his good, pleasing, and perfect will.*

*Romans 12:2 NIV*

**GOD is downright committed to your well-being, your perception of that will determine your acceptance.**

*Therefore, get rid of all moral filth and the evil that is so prevalent and humbly accept the word planted in you, which can save you.*

*James 1:21 NIV*

**Shift your perception from your desired outcome to God's spoken WORD over your position.**

*The Spirit gives life; the flesh counts for nothing. The words I have spoken to you—they are full of the Spirit and life.*

*John 6:63 NIV*

**GOD is absolutely committed to your well-being. Keep this in mind, that your perception of "His" commitment will display in your reaction to every test, trial, and command.**

*Consider it pure joy, my brothers and sisters, whenever you face trials of many kinds, because you know that the testing of your faith produces perseverance.*

*James 1:2-3 NIV*

**When you see "You" From the eyes of the word", You will shift!! It will cause you to Believe & Mature.**

*Examine yourselves to see whether you are in the faith; test yourselves. Do you not realize that Christ Jesus is in you—unless, of course, you fail the test?*

*2 Corinthians 13:5 NIV*

**Your story presents the impression of suffering a total loss, from God's view, He just lightened the load.**

*"For my thoughts are not your thoughts,*
*neither are your ways my ways,"*
*declares the Lord.*

*Isaiah 55:8 NIV*

**Your natural viewpoint must be weakened by "Your Obedience"; Favor erupts when " the odds against you" are revealed.**

*He replied, "Blessed rather are those who hear the word of*
*God and obey it."*

*Luke 11:28 NIV*

**Discontinue allowing your eyes to dictate what you believe. The released promises of God spoken over you and to you will never be denied!!!**

*"...so is my word that goes out from my mouth:*
*It will not return to me empty,*
*but will accomplish what I desire*
*and achieve the purpose for which I sent it."*

*Isaiah 55:11 NIV*

**Never choose not to recognize reality, on the contrary, seek to discern the "impossibility" of what your heart and eyes can't understand**

*Jesus looked at them and said, "With man this is impossible, but with God all things are possible."*

*Matthew 19:26 NIV*

## Notes

_____

_____

_____

_____

_____

_____

_____

_____

_____

_____

_____

_____

_____

_____

_____

_____

_____

_____

_____

_____

_____

_____

_____

_____

# POSITION

**Any position that God finds me "in", he must find me "FAITHFUL".**

*"...as you hold firmly to the word of life. And then I will be able to boast on the day of Christ that I did not run or labor in vain."*

*Philippians 2:16 NIV*

**IF I'm on my knees, standing, or on my back, MY position will display my Love and Loyalty.**

*Let love and faithfulness never leave you;*
*bind them around your neck,*
*write them on the tablet of your heart.*

*Proverbs 3:3 NIV*

**You won't remain at the bottom of the mountain and God has placed someone in position to pull or push you to your over the top Victory".**

*Two are better than one,*
*because they have a good return for their labor:*

*Ecclesiastes 4:9 NIV*

**Opportunity is what God is asking for from "You".**

*Here I am! I stand at the door and knock. If anyone hears my voice and opens the door, I will come in and eat with that person, and they with me.*

*Revelation 3:20 NIV*

# Notes

_____

_____

_____

_____

_____

_____

_____

_____

_____

_____

_____

_____

_____

_____

_____

_____

_____

_____

_____

_____

_____

_____

# POWER

**"Greater Glory" protected You because the "Fight" against Your Destiny was "Violent", You are a living testimony of that POWER.**

*No weapon forged against you will prevail,*
*and you will refute every tongue that accuses you.*
*This is the heritage of the servants of the Lord,*
*and this is their vindication from me,"*
*declares the Lord.*

*Isaiah 54:17 NIV*

**Jesus is in charge of the "Recovery Room".**

*When Jesus entered the synagogue leader's house and saw the noisy crowd and people playing pipes, he said, "Go away. The girl is not dead but asleep." But they laughed at him. After the crowd had been put outside, he went in and took the girl by the hand, and she got up.*

*Matthew 9:23-25 NIV*

**Prayer is the believer's most powerful tool to alter the outcome of events and change lives in this world; use it.**

*Therefore, confess your sins to each other and pray for each other so that you may be healed. The prayer of a righteous person is powerful and effective.*

*James 5:16 NIV*

**Difficult days will never tell the real story, only those days that you, "Almost let go, those days where your struggle had you," will tell the real story. And the blessing behind the real story is 'A Witness to Testify go "God's Keeping Power"'.**

*His divine power has given us everything we need for a godly life through our knowledge of him who called us by his own glory and goodness.*

*2 Peter 1:3 NIV*

## Notes

# PRIDE

**Pride creates Barricades!**

*When pride comes, then comes disgrace,*
*but with humility comes wisdom.*

*Proverbs 11:2 NIV*

**"He gave you favor without merit, now become without pride."**

*"Do nothing out of selfish ambition or vain conceit. Rather, in*
*humility value others above yourselves…"*

*Philippians 2:3 NIV*

**"MATURITY acknowledges it's not worth holding onto Pride, but**
**yielding to Understanding when; "your right", is actually wrong."**

*Discretion will protect you,*
*and understanding will guard you.*

*Proverbs 2:11 NIV*

# Notes

_____

_____

_____

_____

_____

_____

_____

_____

_____

_____

_____

_____

_____

_____

_____

_____

_____

_____

_____

# PROCESS

## Process is continual "OBEDIENCE".

*"...but I gave them this command: Obey me, and I will be your God and you will be my people. Walk in obedience to all I command you, that it may go well with you."*

*Jeremiah 7:23 NIV*

## Remain in it, until "YOU ATTAIN" it.

*But as for you, be strong and do not give up, for your work will be rewarded."*

*2 Chronicles 15:7 NIV*

**Just remember, you released into the atmosphere for God's Will to be done, when "His Process" begins, don't pick and choose how, who, what, and when.**

*Father, if you are willing, take this cup from me; yet not my will, but yours be done.*

*Luke 22:42 NIV*

**Never Pass judgment on those in the place called process, because their development will surrender to Greatness.**

*Do not judge by appearances, but judge with right judgment.*

*John 7:24 ESV*

**Enjoy Being "You". Yes, you may have "flaws", nevertheless, it won't change Your Purpose, only the "Process" of development.**

*For we are his workmanship, created in Christ Jesus for good works, which God prepared beforehand, that we should walk in them.*

*Ephesians 2:10 ESV*

**When we are being Perfected to reach destiny; deny aborting the process, don't jump out of the fire, don't lose faith, and stop blaming those that God will use in the development process.**

*Therefore, we do not lose heart. Though outwardly we are wasting away, yet inwardly we are being renewed day by day.*

*2 Corinthians 4:16 NIV*

**(It's) Just a little turbulence, ride it out. If you bail now the process restarts again, until you learn how to hold on.**

*Blessed is the one who perseveres under trial because, having stood the test, that person will receive the crown of life that the Lord has promised to those who love him.*

*James 1:12 NIV*

**As much as you want someone else to go through for you, it won't relinquish you from a place called process for purpose.**

*Strengthening the disciples and encouraging them to remain true to the faith. "We must go through many hardships to enter the kingdom of God," they said.*

*Acts 14:22 NIV*

**How did you think you would go beyond mediocre? Remain in the process!! Don't abort!!! You are "Necessary & Valuable".**

*Let perseverance finish its work so that you may be mature and complete, not lacking anything.*

*James 1:4 NIV*

# Notes

_____

_____

_____

_____

_____

_____

_____

_____

_____

_____

_____

_____

_____

_____

_____

_____

_____

_____

_____

_____

_____

_____

_____

# PROMISE

**Step aside and allow your fears to come face to face with "Faith & Promise".**

*So do not fear, for I am with you;*
*do not be dismayed, for I am your God.*
*I will strengthen you and help you;*
*I will uphold you with my righteous right hand.*

*Isaiah 41:10 NIV*


**God would not allow your chaos to veto the promise.**

*For no matter how many promises God has made, they are "Yes" in Christ. And so through him the "Amen" is spoken by us to the glory of God.*

*2 Corinthians 1:20 NIV*


**When you are expecting to deliver "PROMISE", You will die to some things in order to get to the next level.**

*Therefore, since we have these promises, dear friends, let us purify ourselves from everything that contaminates body and spirit, perfecting holiness out of reverence for God.*

*2 Corinthians 7:1 NIV*

**The "Promise" will manifest itself. "Get Ready".**

*For,*

*"In just a little while,*
*he who is coming will come*
*and will not delay."*

*Hebrews 10:37 NIV*

**A Promise (One that appeared to be impossible) was given to you from God, one that will shift your life, region, and territory.**

*When Abram was ninety-nine years old, the Lord appeared to him and said, "I am God Almighty; walk before me faithfully and be blameless. Then I will make my covenant between me and you and will greatly increase your numbers."*

*Abram fell facedown, and God said to him, "As for me, this is my covenant with you: You will be the father of many nations. No longer will you be called Abram; your name will be Abraham, for I have made you a father of many nations. I will make you very fruitful; I will make nations of you, and kings will come from you. I will establish my covenant as an everlasting covenant between me and you and your descendants after you for the generations to come, to be your God and the God of your descendants after you. The whole land of Canaan, where you now reside as a foreigner, I will give as an everlasting possession to you and your descendants after you; and I will be their God." Then God said to Abraham, "As for you, you must keep my covenant, you and your descendants after you for the generations to come.*

*This is my covenant with you and your descendants after you, the covenant you are to keep: Every male among you shall be circumcised. You are to undergo circumcision, and it will be the sign of the covenant between me and you. For the generations to come every male among you who is eight days old must be circumcised, including those born in your household or bought with money from a foreigner—those who are not your offspring. Whether born in your household or bought with your money, they must be circumcised. My covenant in your flesh is to be an everlasting covenant. Any uncircumcised male, who has not been circumcised in the flesh, will be cut off from his people; he has broken my covenant." God also said to Abraham, "As for Sarai your wife, you are no longer to call her Sarai; her name will be Sarah. I will bless her and will surely give you a son by her. I will bless her so that she will be the mother of nations; kings of peoples will come from her."*

*Genesis 17:1-16 NIV*

**When you are denied access – it's another opportunity.**

*For I know the plans I have for you," declares the Lord, "plans to prosper you and not to harm you, plans to give you hope and a future.*

*Jeremiah 29:11 NIV*

**Reflect on who you are according to God's Promise over your life, and at the same time compare it to "Your dream", "Which is Greater?**

*For my thoughts are not your thoughts,*
*neither are your ways my ways,*
*declares the Lord.*

*Isaiah 55:8 NIV*

**Never allow your vision to override the Promise God made to "YOU".**

*Now faith is confidence in what we hope for and assurance about what we do not see.*

*Hebrews 11:1 NIV*

**Never allow closed doors to shatter your hopes and dreams when you have been promised the entire land.**

*You need to persevere so that when you have done the will of God, you will receive what he has promised.*

*Hebrews 10:36 NIV*

**God has promised to Honor & Restore You; the facts are not Final.**

*And after you have suffered a little while, the God of all grace, who has called you to his eternal glory in Christ, will himself restore, confirm, strengthen, and establish you.*

*1 Peter 5:10 ESV*

**Don't yield to the voice of despair while you are giving birth to the promise.**

*Let us not become weary in doing good, for at the proper time we will reap a harvest if we do not give up.*

*Galatians 6:9 NIV*

**The purpose of God's promises is to enable us to become more like His Son in our character.**

*Through these he has given us his very great and precious promises, so that through them you may participate in the divine nature, having escaped the corruption in the world caused by evil desires.*

*2 Peter 1:4 NIV*

**The promises are the foundation and the anchor of our life lived in Christ.**

*Know therefore that the Lord your God is God; he is the faithful God, keeping his covenant of love to a thousand generations of those who love him and keep his commandments.*

*Deuteronomy 7:9 NIV*

**Do you want your delivery through His promise or your plan?**

*For I know the plans I have for you, declares the Lord, "plans to prosper you and not to harm you, plans to give you hope and a future.*

*Jeremiah 29:11 NIV*

# Notes

_____

_____

_____

_____

_____

_____

_____

_____

_____

_____

_____

_____

_____

_____

_____

_____

_____

_____

_____

_____

_____

_____

_____

_____

_____

_____

_____

_____

_____

_____

_____

_____

_____

_____

_____

_____

_____

_____

_____

_____

_____

_____

_____

_____

# PURPOSE

**God's Favor and Honor are going to change your "Insecurities" into a Successful story.**

*In him we were also chosen, having been predestined according to the plan of him who works out everything in conformity with the purpose of his will,*

*Ephesians 1:11 NIV*

**Never override purpose!!**

*Many are the plans in a person's heart,*
*but it is the Lord's purpose that prevails.*

*Proverbs 19:21 NIV*

**Purpose has been functioning as your midwife, every time you thought you were ready to deliver, Purpose reminded you, (No-go back), That dream is still in development, go-back, you are still maturing to be able to handle the plan.**

*"Humble yourselves, therefore, under the mighty hand of God so that at the proper time he may exalt you..."*

*1 Peter 5:6 ESV*

**Stop trying to PROVE wrong what people are saying about you and "LIVE" to PROVE right what God has declared over "YOUR" life.**

*Am I now trying to win the approval of human beings, or of God? Or am I trying to please people? If I were still trying to please people, I would not be a servant of Christ.*

*Galatians 1:10 NIV*

**"You can't forget your past, however, your past can serve as a training tool for your Purpose."**

*Only be careful, and watch yourselves closely so that you do not forget the things your eyes have seen or let them fade from your heart as long as you live. Teach them to your children and to their children after them.*

*Deuteronomy 4:9 NIV*

**One of the most difficult things in life to attempt is: Putting forth all your effort to become who you were "NOT" created to "BE". It recreates a distorted self-view of reality and propels you into the opposite direction of purpose.**

*"Before I formed you in the womb I knew you, before you were born I set you apart; I appointed you as a prophet to the nations."*

*Jeremiah 1:5 NIV*

**I WILL become, I CAN achieve, AND I SHALL walk in my purpose.**

*I can do all this through him who gives me strength.*

*Philippians 4:13 NIV*


**"Your" Purpose is calling for "You" to make the next "STEP".**

*Jesus said to him, "Get up, take up your bed, and walk."*

*John 5:8 ESV*


**You were created and destined to live a phenomenal life. Believe and Respond", Let the Mundane and Mediocre life Go.**

*And God is able to bless you abundantly, so that in all things at all times, having all that you need, you will abound in every good work.*

*2 Corinthians 9:8 NIV*


**"Purpose motivated by "Something" determines Your Walk."**

*Whatever you do, work at it with all your heart, as working for the Lord, not for human masters,*

*Colossians 3:23 NIV*

**By no means; allow anyone to keep you from your purpose, even when your eyes can't see your future and when your heart wishes to give up.**

*My flesh and my heart may fail,*
*but God is the strength of my heart and my portion forever.*

*Psalm 73:26 ESV*

**Walk in it. God knew who He was choosing!!!**

*For those God foreknew he also predestined to be conformed to the image of his Son, that he might be the firstborn among many brothers and sisters. And those he predestined, he also called; those he called, he also justified; those he justified, he also glorified.*

*Romans 8:29-30 NIV*

**When "WAR FLESH" released a path of devastation in your life, God Declared an "Emergency STAY", you won't abort "HIS PURPOSE".**

*The Lord is a refuge for the oppressed,*
*a stronghold in times of trouble.*
*Those who know your name trust in you,*
*for you, Lord, have never forsaken those who seek you.*

*Psalm 9:9-10 NIV*

**If I take my King for His Word, exercise kingdom principles; it will produce a Kingdom minded citizen that will live out his/her purpose; not problem free, but free to "Be".**

*Blessed are those whose ways are blameless,*
*who walk according to the law of the Lord.*
*Blessed are those who keep his statutes*
*and seek him with all their heart—*
*they do no wrong*
*but follow his ways.*

*Psalm 119:1-3 NIV*

**Whenever God gives you an assignment, He takes away the leverage the enemy has against you.**

*And we know that all things work together for good to them that love God, to them who are the called according to his purpose.*

*Romans 8:28 KJV*

**You were chosen. Must we see the entire picture in order to follow faithfully?**

*But you are a chosen race, a royal priesthood, a holy nation, a people for his own possession, that you may proclaim the excellencies of him who called you out of darkness into his marvelous light.*

*1 Peter 2:9 ESV*

**If you don't understand your Purpose, you will operate outside your divine destiny.**

*The Lord said to Joshua, "Do not be afraid of them; I have given them into your hand. Not one of them will be able to withstand you."*

*Joshua 10:8 NIV*

# Notes

_____

_____

_____

_____

_____

_____

_____

_____

_____

_____

_____

_____

_____

_____

_____

_____

_____

_____

_____

_____

_____

_____

_____

_____

# ABOUT THE AUTHOR

Melinda is a wife, grandmother, mom, and Pastor. As a mother of five (Allen, Tiffany, Shana, Courtney, and Orlando), and grandmother of four one of her greatest joys is spending time with her family and sowing into their continued development. Several years ago, her youngest son Orlando purchased two pit bull dogs. Upon their first introduction, Melinda's love for her family extended to Landis and Blu who she lovingly calls her "grandpups". Each time they see her they greet her with love, hugs and kisses that are nothing short of memorable. Orlando recently added Luna and Medusa to the "grandpups" tribe. Now, there is double the love and double the fun.

Melinda can never truly be described completely without telling of her unwavering love and commitment to Jesus Christ. As a young disciple Melinda sought to know and follow Christ with her entire being. She understands and yields completely to the principles of followship, righteousness, love, and truth. Ask anyone that knows her, and you will receive a clear account of a woman that loves God and extends it without partiality to all people. In 2007, Melinda was installed as Pastor of Bethlehem Baptist Church of Tallahassee. Now named Divine Glory Ministries, Inc., Apostle Sutton has led the ministry under the guidance, leadership, and covering of God and trusted persons of faith. After 12 years of leadership, she has learned countless lessons that have further strengthened her love and commitment to her heavenly father, Jesus Christ. She serves as a living witness to the power of God that is active in all things.

After many years, tears, triumph, and perseverance Melinda is at a pivotal point to continue yet another leg of her journey in the faith. She is humbled, ecstatic, and grateful to be chosen by God to be used of him. Look out and look up. There is more on the horizon!!